Maraya Clark

PRENTICE HALL
Realidades

Video Workbook
¿Eres tú, María?

PEARSON

Prentice
Hall

Boston, Massachusetts
Upper Saddle River, New Jersey

Marsha Clark

Acknowledgments

"¿Eres tú, María?" is based on the novél *¿Eres tú, María?* (from the *"Lola Lago, Detective"* séries) by Lourdes Miguel
and Neus Sans, Difusíon centro de Investigación y Publicaciones de Idiomas, S.L. Barcelona, Spain, 1998.

Copyright © by Pearson Education, Inc., publishing as Pearson Prentice Hall, Boston, Massachusetts 02116.
All rights reserved. Printed in the United States of America. This publication is protected by copyright, and permission should be obtained from the publisher prior to any prohibited reproduction, storage in a retrieval system, or
transmission in any form or by any means, electronic, mechanical, photocopying, recording, or likewise. For
information regarding permission(s), write to: Rights and Permissions Department.

Pearson Prentice Hall™ is a trademark of Pearson Education, Inc.
Pearson® is a registered trademark of Pearson plc.
Prentice Hall® is a registered trademark of Pearson Education, Inc.

9 10   08

ISBN 0-13-036050-3

Realidades 1

Episodio 1

Nombre _____

Hora _____

Fecha _____

EPISODIO 1

Antes de ver el video

Resumen del episodio

Lola Lago es una detective privada que trabaja en Madrid, la capital de España. Es la una de la mañana y Lola está en su piso. Desde su balcón ve a dos personas hablando enfrente de un edificio.[1] Ella va a la calle[2] y encuentra[3] algo muy importante. Al día siguiente[4] doña Lupe, la portera del edificio, va al piso de doña Gracia y . . .

[1] building [2] street [3] finds [4] The next day

Personajes

Lola Lago es detective privada.

Doña Lupe es portera de un edificio.

Doña Gracia es residente de un piso.

Vocabulario

las llaves   keys
el periódico   newspaper
el piso   apartment; floor (of a building)
la portera   doorkeeper; in Spain, a person who watches over a building in exchange for a small salary and free apartment

© Pearson Education, Inc. All rights reserved.

Realidades ❶

Episodio 1

Nombre _____

Fecha _____

Hora _____

EPISODIO 1

Para pensar

Discuss the following themes with other students:

1. If you were going to spend several weeks abroad, would you like to visit a large city like Madrid, or would you prefer to spend your time in the country? Explain your choices, citing the pros and cons of each type of place.

2. What requirements do you think a person needs to become a private detective? Does this career appeal to you? Why or why not?

Para observar

In this episode, you're going to see the interior of Lola's apartment. Think about how it might be the same or different from your house or apartment and pay attention to what is there.

Después de ver el video

¿Qué observas?

A. Check off all of the following items that appeared in Lola's apartment.

1. __✓__ el teléfono

2. __✓__ las plantas

3. __✓__ el sofá

4. __✓__ la mesa

5. __✓__ los libros

6. __✓__ la silla

7. _____ el refrigerador

8. _____ las llaves

9. __✓__ las fotografías

10. __✓__ las lámparas

© Pearson Education, Inc. All rights reserved.

B. Think about what you thought Lola's apartment might be like. Were your predictions correct? How is her home the same or different from yours?

_____

_____

_____

¿Comprendes?

A. Who does each statement describe: Lola, doña Lupe, or doña Gracia? Write the correct name or names next to each statement.

_____Lola_____ **1.** Es una detective joven.

_____Doña lupe_____ **2.** Es portera.

_____Doña Gracia_____ **3.** Su casa está en la Plaza del Alamillo, número 8.

_____Doña Lupe_____ **4.** Tiene el periódico de doña Gracia.

_____Lola_____ **5.** Compra (She buys) un periódico de Gabriel.

B. Match each quotation below to a scene from the video by writing the letter of the appropriate scene in the blank provided.

a.  b.  c.  d.

__C__ **1.** "Sí, es un día fantástico. *El País,* por favor. Un euro, ¿no?"

__A__ **2.** "Uf, es la una."

__B__ **3.** "Unas llaves . . . y . . . J.R.D."

__D__ **4.** "Por favor. Necesito una ambulancia. Plaza del Alamillo, número 8. Tercer piso. Rápido."

© Pearson Education, Inc. All rights reserved.

C. Read each sentence below and write *C* (*cierto*) if it is true and *F* (*falso*) if it is false. If it is false, write the correct information on the line.

1. Es sábado, el 15 de octubre. __F__ _____

2. Son las dos de la mañana. __C__ _____

3. Lola compra *(buys)* el periódico *ABC*. __C__ _____

4. Doña Lupe es portera. __C__ _____

5. Lola Lago es detective privada. __C__ _____

6. Lola necesita ir en una ambulancia. __F__ _____

7. Doña Lupe encuentra unas llaves. __C__ _____

D. Circle the letter (*A* or *B*) of the correct phrase in each pair.

1. **(A)** Doña Lupe ve a dos personas hablando.
   B. Lola Lago ve a dos personas hablando.

2. **A.** Doña Lupe tiene el periódico de Lola.
   (B.) Doña Lupe tiene el periódico de doña Gracia.

3. **(A.)** Doña Lupe necesita a la policía.
   B. Doña Lupe necesita una ambulancia.

4. **A.** Lola va al piso de doña Gracia.
   (B.) Doña Lupe va al piso de doña Gracia.

5. **(A.)** Es la una de la mañana cuando Lola va a su piso.
   B. Es la una de la tarde cuando Lola va a su piso.

6. **A.** El sábado, a las nueve de la mañana, Lola sale de *(leaves)* su piso.
   (B.) El domingo, a las diez de la mañana, Lola sale de su piso.

© Pearson Education, Inc. All rights reserved.

Para hablar

You and a partner are talking at a newsstand in Spanish. One of you is the newspaper vendor and the other is a customer. The vendor starts the conversation. Use a real newspaper prop to make your conversation more authentic.

The vendor:

• Greet the customer. Ask how he or she is.

• Answer the customer's question.

• Give the customer the newspaper and state the price in euros.

• Say you're welcome and goodbye

The customer:

• Greet the vendor, answer his or her question, and ask how he or she is.

• Ask for the daily newspaper; don't forget to say please.

• Pay for it and say thank you.

© Pearson Education, Inc. All rights reserved.

Para escribir

Pretend you are Lola Lago and you are trying to find more clients for your business. Write a three-sentence newspaper ad to help attract clients. You might use some of these sentence starters:

> Me llamo . . .
> Soy . . . .
> Me gusta . . .
> Me gustaría . . .
> Me encanta . . .

Para decir más

el cliente, la clienta   client
el crimen   crime
Quiero investigar . . .   I want to investigate . . .

© Pearson Education, Inc. All rights reserved.

Nota cultural

El teléfono

People answer the phone differently in different places. *Hola* might be heard in any Spanish-speaking country. *Bueno* is used in México. In Cuba people say *¿Qué hay?* and *Oigo*. *A ver* is heard in Colombia. People answer the phone with *Aló* in Peru and Ecuador. *Al habla* and *Al aparato* are used in several countries.

In Spain people answer the telephone with *Dígame, Diga, Dime,* or *¿Sí?*

What does Lola say when she answers the phone? _____

How do you answer the telephone? _____

Compare your answer with those of other classmates. What is the most common way

to answer the phone? _____

Is it unusual to get a phone call at 1 A.M. at your house? _____

Why or why not? _____

© Pearson Education, Inc. All rights reserved.

Realidades 1

Episodio 1

Nombre _____

Fecha _____

Hora _____

EPISODIO 1

Nota cultural

Don y doña

The words *don* (used in addressing a man) and *doña* (used in addressing a woman) are titles of respect in Spanish that have no equivalents in English. They are commonly used and written in lower case unless they are abbreviated. The abbreviations for *don* (D.) and *doña* (D.ª) are always capitalized.

Don and *doña* are used before a person's first name, whether or not it is followed by the last name:
Don Miguel está aquí. D. Miguel Sánchez está aquí.
Doña María es mi profesora. D.ª María Castro es mi profesora.

Don and *doña* are used without the last name to show respect and closeness when talking to someone:
¿Cómo está, don Miguel?
Doña Isabel, ¿cómo está su familia?

Which title is used in *Episodio* 1? _____

Who does the name refer to? _____

What titles of respect are used in your community? _____

_____

© Pearson Education, Inc. All rights reserved.

Realidades 1

Episodio 1

Nombre

Fecha

Hora

EPISODIO 1

Para explorar en Internet

Lola buys a popular Spanish newspaper, *El País*. Go online to find two other newspapers from Spain. Scan the papers for some articles and see how much you can understand. Remember to look for cognates. How do these newspapers compare to those you and your family read?

_____

_____

_____

_____

_____

_____

© Pearson Education, Inc. All rights reserved.

Nombre _____   Hora _____

Fecha _____   **EPISODIO 2**

Antes de ver el video

Resumen del episodio

En este episodio, la ambulancia llega¹ y lleva² a doña Gracia al hospital. También llegan dos inspectores de policía. Hablan con doña Lupe, la portera, sobre el incidente en el piso de doña Gracia. Lola se presenta³ a los dos hombres y les dice⁴ lo que sabe del incidente.

¹ arrives   ² takes (away)   ³ introduces herself   ⁴ tells them

Personajes

 El inspector Gil es inspector de policía.

 El inspector Peña también es inspector de policía.

Vocabulario

anoche   last night
ayudar   to help
esperar   to wait
¿Quién era?   Who was she?
saber   to know
la sobrina   niece
vi (*ver*)   I saw (*to see*)
vive (*vivir*)   she lives (*to live*)

Frases importantes

No sé.   I don't know.

M2079NX

© Pearson Education, Inc. All rights reserved.

Para pensar

Cognates *(Cognados)* are words that look alike and have similar meanings in English and Spanish. You will usually be able to guess the meaning of cognates easily. Becoming skilled at recognizing cognates will help you understand what you read and increase your vocabulary. Here are some cognates that are used in the first two episodes of the video. Write the English equivalent next to each one.

el inspector _____   la ambulancia _____

el policía _____   la detective _____

horrible _____   la descripción _____

el crimen _____   el hospital _____

la víctima _____   la plaza _____

rápido _____   personas _____

contento _____   clientes _____

magnífico _____

Para observar

You will see an ambulance in this episode. As you watch the video, pay attention to its license plate. How is it different from an American license plate?

Después de ver el video

¿Qué observas?

Did you notice the license plate of the ambulance? What is the first letter? _____

What do you suppose it stands for? _____

Is there a system for assigning license plates where you live? Briefly describe this system.

_____

_____

_____

© Pearson Education, Inc. All rights reserved.

¿Comprendes?

A. Read each description and decide which character it describes. Write the name of the appropriate person in the blank.

1. Es la sobrina de doña Gracia y vive con ella. _María_____

2. Vive en el tercer piso en la Plaza del Alamillo y es la víctima. _Doña Gracia_____

3. Es el inspector de policía con el pelo castaño. _Gil_____

4. Es el inspector de policía con poco pelo. _Peña_____

5. Es detective privada y vive en la Plaza del Alamillo. _Lola_____

6. Ella es portera del edificio de doña Gracia. _Doña Lupe_____

© Pearson Education, Inc. All rights reserved.

Realidades ①

Episodio 2

Nombre _____

Fecha _____

Hora _____

EPISODIO 2

B. Circle the letter of the sentence that best describes each scene from the video.

1.
A. Doña Gracia y Lola hablan enfrente de su piso.
B. Doña Lupe y Lola hablan enfrente de su piso.

2.
A. Sí, soy detective privada. Pero, a la una de la mañana, es imposible ver mucho.
B. Sí, soy detective privada. Pero, a las dos de la tarde, es imposible ver mucho.

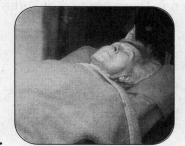

3.
A. Es María, la hija del hermano de su esposo.
B. Es doña Gracia. Vive en el tercer piso.

4.
A. ¿Usted vive aquí? ¿Quién es la víctima?
B. ¿Y es Ud. dectective privada?

© Pearson Education, Inc. All rights reserved.

Realidades ❶

Episodio 2

Nombre _____

Fecha _____

Hora _____

EPISODIO 2

C. Read each sentence and write *C* (*cierto*) if it is true and *F* (*falso*) if it is false. If it is false, write the correct information on the line.

1. Doña Gracia vive en el primer piso. _F_____

2. La ambulancia lleva a doña Gracia al hotel. ___F_____

3. Doña Lupe es detective privada. _F_____

4. El inspector Peña es inspector de policía. __C_____

5. A la una de la mañana, doña Lupe vio a un hombre y a una mujer. _F_____

   _____

6. Lola y doña Gracia leen el periódico *El País.* _F_____

7. Doña Lupe es la víctima del crimen. ___F_____

D. Write the numbers of the phrases that describe each character. There are two or three phrases for each character, and some phrases are used more than once.

_2,3,8_   _6,7_   _1,2,4_   _5,8_

✓ **1.** Va al hospital en ambulancia.

✓ **2.** Vive en la Plaza del Alamillo.

✓ **3.** Es detective privada.

✓ **4.** Vive en el número 8, tercer piso.

✓ **5.** Es policía.

✓ **6.** Trabaja en la Plaza del Alamillo.

✓ **7.** Tiene el periódico de doña Gracia.

✓ **8.** Investiga el crimen.

© Pearson Education, Inc. All rights reserved.

Realidades 1

Episodio 2

Nombre _____

Hora _____

Fecha _____

EPISODIO 2

Nota cultural

Tarjetas de visita

Lola and Inspector Gil exchange business or calling cards, *tarjetas de visita*, a common practice in Spanish-speaking countries. Businessmen and women may have cards they use in social situations, as well as in their business dealings.

Make your own *tarjeta de visita* to share with other students. You may use an index card your teacher will give you to do this. Write your name as if you were in a Spanish-speaking country, and include both your father's and your mother's last name. Include your address (plus an e-mail address), telephone number, and your future profession if one appeals to you. You may choose from the following list. Notice how many of the words are cognates: *profesor(a), secretario(a), fotógrafo(a), doctor(a), arquitecto(a), músico(a), piloto(a), carpintero(a)*

Here are some examples:

Gloria Muñoz Pradera
Fotógrafa

calle Alcalá 203, 4° B
28033 Madrid   91 576 45 67

Miguel Fernández Ochoa
Presidente
Academia Ochoa

calle Mayor 5, 2°
28005 Madrid   91 366 52 16

© Pearson Education, Inc. All rights reserved.

Realidades ❶

Episodio 2

Nombre _____

Fecha _____

Hora _____

EPISODIO 2

👥 Para hablar

Lola Lago

Use your *tarjeta de visita* to have a conversation among your classmates. Introduce yourself and exchange cards with five other students.

Estudiante A:

• Greet a student and introduce yourself. Ask the student his or her name.

• Tell the student how you are and ask for his or her address and telephone number.

• Thank the student and give him or her the information and your card. Say you're glad to meet him or her.

Estudiante B:

• Answer the student's question. Then ask him or her how he or she is. _____

_____

• Tell the student your address and phone number and give him or her your card. Ask for the student's address and phone number.

_____

_____

_____

• Thank the student and say you're glad to meet him or her.

_____

© Pearson Education, Inc. All rights reserved.

Realidades ❶

Episodio 2

Nombre _____

Fecha _____

Hora _____

EPISODIO 2

Para decir más

¿Cuál es tu dirección (electrónica)?
    What's your (e-mail) address?
¿Cuál es tu número de teléfono?
    What's your phone number?

 ## Para escribir

Pretend you are Lola. Write a short note in Spanish to police inspectors Gil and Peña, offering to help them find the person responsible for the crime against doña Gracia.

Para decir más

ayudar   to help
investigar   to investigate
me gustaría   I would like
quiero   I want

You might begin: *Me llamo Lola Lago y soy detective privada. Me gustaría . . .*

_____

_____

_____

_____

_____

_____

© Pearson Education, Inc. All rights reserved.

Nota cultural

Los pisos

Piso means "floor" or "story". In Spain, the ground floor is the *planta baja (P.B.)* or the *piso bajo* (also *P.B.*) The next floor is *el primer piso* (first floor, first story), and the one after that is *el segundo piso* (second floor, second story).

Doña Gracia lives on *el tercer piso.* What floor is that in the American floor-numbering system?

_____

© Pearson Education, Inc. All rights reserved.

Realidades 1

Episodio 2

Nombre _____

Hora _____

Fecha _____

EPISODIO 2

Para explorar en Internet

Lola waits for Inspectors Gil and Peña in the plaza. A *plaza* is an open square surrounded by buildings and is the social center of the neighborhood in Spanish-speaking countries. Go online to discover interesting facts about Madrid's most famous plaza: *la Plaza Mayor*. Write a few facts about its history. Then, describe five things you might find there, as well as five activities that traditionally go on in *la Plaza Mayor*.

_____

_____

_____

_____

_____

_____

_____

_____

_____

_____

_____

© Pearson Education, Inc. All rights reserved.

Antes de ver el video

Resumen del episodio

Este episodio es muy importante. Lola le explica a Paco lo que pasó[1] en el incidente del domingo pasado.[2] En otra escena, doña Lupe le describe a Lola el incidente en el piso de doña Gracia. Doña Lupe también le explica a Lola la historia de la familia de doña Gracia. ¿Por qué cree que María va a recibir toda la fortuna de doña Gracia?

[1]what happened   [2]last Sunday

Personajes

Paco es detective privado y trabaja con Lola. La ayuda con las investigaciones.

Margarita es la secretaria de la oficina.

Vocabulario

abro   I open
el accidente de coche   car accident
busco   I look for
el dinero   money
las joyas   jewels
muerto, -a   dead
el nieto   grandson
el / la periodista   newspaper reporter
¿Robaron . . . ?   Did they steal . . . ?

© Pearson Education, Inc. All rights reserved.

Realidades ❶

Episodio 3

Nombre _____

Fecha _____

Hora _____

EPISODIO 3

Frases importantes

Él no conoce a su abuela.   He doesn't know his grandmother.
No ve casi nada.   She can hardly see anything.
No viene nunca aquí.   He never comes here.
Pasó antes de venir a vivir con   It happened before she came to live
   doña Gracia.   with doña Gracia.
Pasó tres meses . . .   She spent three months . . .
¿Qué pasó?   What happened?

Para pensar

In this episode, Lola tells her colleague Paco that she is going home to have lunch and take a nap *(una siesta)*. Discuss with other students why you think this custom is popular in Spain. Is a *siesta* a common practice where you live? Who usually takes naps? Is this a custom or habit that you would like to have? Why or why not? Would it be compatible with school or work schedules in your community? Why or why not?

Para observar

As you watch the video, listen for an English word that Paco uses. Then, listen closely to an expression that Lupe uses and a sign that she makes when she is talking to Lola.

Después de ver el video

¿Qué observas?

1. What is the English word that Paco used? _____hover_____ What does he mean by this? _you have to get money to do the job_ It's not yet a hobbie to do when you want to. Why do you think he is upset with Lola? _Because she is getting h to something she shouldn't_ _by a person who won't her client e wasn't paid._

2. While Lola and Lupe are talking, Lupe makes the sign of the cross and says *"que en paz descanse."* What does this mean and who is she referring to? _____

_____

The Spanish abbreviation of this expression is *QEPD* and it is commonly found on tombstones in the Spanish-speaking world. What is the English abbreviation of this saying? _____RIP_____

© Pearson Education, Inc. All rights reserved.

Realidades ①

Episodio 3

Nombre _____

Fecha _____

Hora _____

EPISODIO 3

¿Comprendes?

A. Who does each sentence describe: Lola, Margarita, Paco, María, or doña Lupe?

Lola   **1.** Es modelo profesional.

Doña Lupe   **2.** Sabe mucho de doña Gracia.

Margarita   **3.** Es secretaria en la oficina de Lola.

Paco   **4.** Es detective y trabaja con Lola.

Lola   **5.** Dice que es periodista.

B. Choose the number of the sentence that corresponds to each scene from the video and write it in the appropriate blank. One scene has two correct answers.

   _2,5_

   _1_

   _3,4_

   _____

1. Lola, si no hay cliente, si no hay dinero, entonces no hay nada.

2. Me encantan los secretos.

3. Pero primero, voy a casa a comer y a dormir una siesta.

4. Disculpa. Perdón.

5. Pues, creo que María va a recibir toda la fortuna.

22   *Episodio 3* ━ *¿Eres tú, María?*

© Pearson Education, Inc. All rights reserved.

C. Lola is very busy. Put her activities in chronological order by writing *1* next to the first thing she did and *6* next to the last thing she did.

_____ **1.** Habla con doña Lupe.

_____ **2.** Va a su oficina.

_____ **3.** Va a su piso a comer y dormir una siesta.

_____ **4.** Come una manzana.

_____ **5.** Habla con Margarita.

_____ **6.** Habla con Paco.

D. Circle the letter (*A* or *B*) of the phrase that best completes each sentence. Then, draw a line from the sentence to the photo it corresponds to.

1. Margarita, la secretaria de la oficina,

   A. trabaja mucho.
   B. habla mucho por teléfono.

2. Dice que si no hay cliente, no hay

   A. problema.
   B. dinero.

3. Lola y Lupe

   A. hablan en el piso.
   B. hablan en la plaza.

4. Lola le dice a doña Lupe que es

   A. detective.
   B. periodista.

© Pearson Education, Inc. All rights reserved.

Realidades ❶

Episodio 3

Nombre _____

Fecha _____

Hora _____

EPISODIO 3

 Para hablar

With a partner, replay the conversation between Lola and Lupe in front of Lupe's building. One of you will play the part of Lola, the other will be doña Lupe.

Lola:

• Ask Lupe about doña Gracia's condition.

• Ask who else lives in doña Gracia's apartment.

Doña Lupe:

• Reply that doña Gracia is in a coma in the hospital San Carlos. She's 85 years old and does not see very well.

• Say that her niece María lives there but isn't there now. Explain that María will receive doña Gracia's money and jewels.

Then, switch roles to practice both parts. Present your conversation to the rest of the class.

Para decir más

¿Cómo está doña Gracia?   How is doña Gracia?
las joyas   the jewels
No puede ver bien.   She can't see well.
su sobrina   her niece
Tiene 85 años.   She's 85 years old.
Va a recibir . . .   She's going to receive . . .

© Pearson Education, Inc. All rights reserved.

Realidades 1

Episodio 3

Nombre _____

Fecha _____

Hora _____

EPISODIO 3

Para escribir

Pretend you are Lola. Write a five-sentence postcard to your friend in the United States. Describe your work, your coworkers, your apartment, and Madrid.

Para decir más

trabajar   to work
vivir   to live

Nota cultural

Madrid

Lola Lago lives and works in downtown Madrid, the capital of and largest city in Spain. Madrid is located in the geographical center of the country, and has a population of about 3 million people. It has been the capital since 1561. Like many other European cities, Madrid is a combination of the old and the new. It has structures that date from the 1600s as well as impressive skyscrapers and stylish new hotels. In the older sections of the city—where Lola and doña Lupe live—you can still find quiet little plazas, narrow streets, and buildings usually no taller than five stories. The "new" Madrid has spacious public squares, wider boulevards, and tall, modern buildings.

La Gran Vía is one of the city's main shopping districts as well as a popular tourist attraction, with its many hotels, movie theaters, restaurants, and cafés. At the end of this broad avenue is *la Plaza de España*. In addition to gardens and outdoor cafés, this famous spot also has a statue of don Quijote and Sancho Panza, the fictitious characters made famous by Miguel de Cervantes in his novel *Don Quijote*, published in 1605. Don Quijote is a dreamer and idealist who goes on a quest to right the wrongs of the world. In his adventures, he is ready to slay giants and rescue damsels in distress. His faithful squire Sancho Panza is a practical man who tries to protect his master from danger.

If you were going to design a plaza for your community, who would you choose as a model for a statue? Why?

_____

_____

_____

© Pearson Education, Inc. All rights reserved.

Realidades ❶

Episodio 3

Nombre _____

Hora _____

Fecha _____

EPISODIO 3

Para explorar en Internet

Go online to find out some more interesting facts about *la Plaza de España*. What else did you find out?

_____

_____

_____

_____

_____

_____

_____

_____

_____

_____

_____

_____

_____

_____

© Pearson Education, Inc. All rights reserved.

Realidades 1

Episodio 4

Nombre _____

Fecha _____

Hora _____

EPISODIO 4

Antes de ver el video

Resumen del episodio

Doña Gracia está mucho mejor y puede ir a casa en unos días, pero no recuerda mucho del incidente. Lola llama por teléfono a su buena amiga, Carmela. Las dos van a un café para hablar y Carmela le dice a Lola que una de sus amigas, Rosalinda, trabaja en el Hospital San Carlos. Es el hospital donde está doña Gracia. Deciden ir al hospital para hablar con Rosalinda y ver a doña Gracia. A la mañana siguiente,* Lola habla con Pedro Requena, el nieto de doña Gracia.

*next

Personajes

Carmela es una buena amiga de Lola.

Pedro Requena es el nieto de doña Gracia y vive en Italia.

Vocabulario

ahora mismo   right away
los churros   fried dough pastries
el golpe   hit; blow
preguntar por   to ask about
¿Sabe . . . ?   Does she know . . . ?

Frases importantes

¿Habló del incidente?   Did she talk about the incident?
No estoy pensando en . . .   I'm not planning to . . .
Sólo recuerda . . .   She only remembers . . .
Voy a pensarlo.   I'll think about it.
Yo fui a visitarla.   I went to visit her.

© Pearson Education, Inc. All rights reserved.

Realidades ①

Nombre _____

Hora _____

Episodio 4

Fecha _____

EPISODIO 4

Para pensar

Spaniards often prefer getting together with friends at a café, rather than at home. Why do you think they prefer this? Where do you and your friends like meeting: at someone's home, or at some public place? Why do you prefer this meeting place? What would be the advantages and disadvantages of both of these meeting places? Discuss this with other students.

Para observar

In this episode, Lola meets her friend Carmela at the café Barbieri and the next morning Lola goes to the same café by herself. Pay attention to what is ordered each time.

Después de ver el video

¿Qué observas?

What did Lola and her friend Carmela order to drink at the Café Barbieri? What do you think *"con gas"* means? What did they order for a snack *(una tapa)?* _y agua con gas_

Lola + her friend ordered cafe con leche, una tortilla for
snack. "con gas" mean w/ bubbles. (something)

What does Lola have the next morning? How is this similar to, or different from, what you usually have for breakfast?

for breakfast Lola has cafe con leche y los churros. usually
I don't have churros for breakfast is more of a treat for
lunch.

¿Comprendes?

A. Circle the letter of the word or words that best complete each sentence.

1. La secretaria de la oficina se llama
   - **a.** María.
   - **b.** Magdalena. ✓
   - **c.** Margarita. ⟲

2. Paco es
   - **a.** detective. ⟲
   - **b.** profesor. ✓
   - **c.** secretario.

© Pearson Education, Inc. All rights reserved.

Realidades ①

Episodio 4

Nombre _____

Fecha _____

Hora _____

EPISODIO 4

3. Si no hay _____, no hay dinero.

   a. hombre

   b. cliente

   c. comida

4. Lola Lago no es

   a. periodista.

   b. detective.

   c. mujer.

5. Doña Gracia está

   a. bien.

   b. mejor.

   c. ocupada.

6. La mejor amiga de Lola es

   a. Margarita.

   b. Rosalinda.

   c. Carmela.

7. Lola y Carmela están en

   a. una oficina.

   b. un café.

   c. un hotel.

8. El hospital se llama

   a. San Felipe.

   b. San Carlos.

   c. Santa María.

9. _____ trabaja en el hospital.

   a. Margarita

   b. Rosalinda

   c. Carmela

© Pearson Education, Inc. All rights reserved.

Realidades 1

Episodio 4

Nombre _____

Fecha _____

Hora _____

EPISODIO 4

B. Answer the following questions in complete sentences.

1. ¿Por qué dice Paco que no pueden trabajar? _____
   _____

2. ¿Con quién habla Lola enfrente de su piso? _____

3. ¿Quién está mejor? _____

4. ¿Quién es la mejor amiga de Lola? _____

5. ¿Dónde están Lola y su amiga? ¿Qué hacen allí?
   _____

6. ¿Qué es la buena idea de Carmela?
   _____

7. ¿Adónde va Lola al día siguiente por la mañana? _____

8. ¿Con quién habla Lola allí? _____

9. ¿A quién llama Pedro por teléfono? _____

C. Draw a line from each scene to the phrase that best describes it.

1. Doña Lupe le dice a Lola que doña Gracia puede venir a casa en unos días.

2. Lola y Carmela van a pedir algo en el Café Barbieri.

3. Lola le pide al camarero un café con leche y churros también.

4. Lola le da a Pedro su número de teléfono.

© Pearson Education, Inc. All rights reserved.

Realidades ❶

Episodio 4

Nombre _____

Hora _____

Fecha _____

EPISODIO 4

 Para hablar

You're in Madrid and it's time for a hot or cold drink and *una tapa.* Work with a partner and prepare a conversation that you'll present to the rest of the class. Remember that in Spain, the customer has to ask for the check when he or she is ready to pay; the waiter will seldom bring the check unless it is requested.

El (la) camarero(a):

• Greet the customer. Ask what he or she wants to drink.

• Ask if the customer is going to eat something.

• Serve the customer and present the check when asked. Thank the customer.

El cliente / la clienta:

• Greet the *camarero(a).* Order something to drink.

• Ask for *una tapa de tortilla, churros,* or anything else from the menu.

• Thank the *camarero(a)* when your order served.

• Ask for the check and say thank you.

Para decir más

La cuenta, por favor.   The check, please.
¿Qué desea beber?   What do you want to drink?
Quisiera . . .   I would like . . .
¿Va a comer algo?   Are you going to eat something?

 Para escribir

Make a menu in Spanish that includes both hot and cold drinks and *tapas.* Headings include: *las bebidas frías, las bebidas calientes,* and *las tapas.* State the prices in euros. Give your café an

© Pearson Education, Inc. All rights reserved.

Realidades 1

Episodio 4

Nombre _____

Fecha _____

Hora _____

EPISODIO 4

Nota cultural

Las tapas

Las tapas are appetizers or small portions of food that can be eaten at any time of day or night. Many Spaniards like going from place to place, enjoying the specialties of each establishment. The *tortilla española* that Lola and Carmela order is nothing like the corn or flour *tortilla* in Mexico. *La tortilla española* is an egg omelette made with potatoes and onions and fried in olive oil. Almost anything could be a tapa, but olives, almonds, assorted seafood, Spanish ham *(jamón serrano),* and a variety of Spanish sausages and cheeses are especially popular. Some cafés may offer up to 100 different kinds of tapas!

The word *tapa* literally means lid or cover. Years ago, the first tapa was a slice of ham that was put over the top of a customer's drink so the flies wouldn't get in. The salty ham made clients thirsty, so owners of these establishments welcomed the tapa as a means to increase business. Thus, the tradition of tapas was born.

Do tapas sound appealing to you? Why or why not? _Yes, because since_
I can never tell what I like e canal always eat
a big plate full of food everyday.
_____

Do you think tapas would be popular in the United States? Why or why not? _____
_____
_____
_____

© Pearson Education, Inc. All rights reserved.

Realidades **1**

Episodio 4

Nombre _____

Hora _____

Fecha _____

EPISODIO 4

Nota cultural

Los churros

One of Spain's favorite breakfast treats and snacks is the *churro,* a batter of flour, salt, and water which is rolled into a tubular circle and then fried. The pastry is then cut into eight-inch pieces, which are often topped with sugar. This great-tasting treat is usually served with hot chocolate so thick it could almost hold a spoon straight up.

One of the most famous places to buy *churros* in Madrid is *la Chocolatería San Ginés,* which opened in 1894. You can ask for a glass of water but you cannot order anything else but *churros y chocolate!*

What do you think is the American equivalent to *churros*? Why? _____

_____

_____

_____

© Pearson Education, Inc. All rights reserved.

Para explorar en Internet

Go online to research some of the more interesting restaurant-cafés in Madrid. A few places to look up include: *Café Gijón, La Bola, Viva Madrid, Café Comercial,* and *El Sobrino del Botín,* which is the oldest restaurant in the world (it opened in 1725).

Antes de ver el video

Resumen del episodio

Lola y Carmela van al hospital para hablar con Rosalinda sobre doña Gracia y María. Descubren[1] más sobre el accidente de coche de María. Ocurrió entre María y otra joven, Julia. Las dos fueron llevadas[2] al Hospital San Carlos. Desafortunadamente,[3] Julia murió. Rosalinda va a los archivos para buscar[4] los historiales clínicos de Julia y María. Pero hay un problema . . .

[1]They find out   [2]were taken   [3]Unfortunately   [4]to look for

Personajes

Rosalinda es una amiga de Carmela y trabaja en el Hospital San Carlos.

Vocabulario

el archivo   record
la carretera   highway
el enfermero   (male) nurse
los historiales clínicos   medical records
murió   died
las visitas   visitors

Frases importantes

Dos coches chocaron . . .   Two cars crashed . . .
Él les ayudó a las dos.   He helped the two of them.
Estuvo aquí . . .   She was here . . .
No viene a trabajar.   He hasn't been coming to work.
Sí, me acuerdo de María.   Yes, I remember María.
¿Te acuerdas de ella?   Do you remember her?

© Pearson Education, Inc. All rights reserved.

Realidades 1

Episodio 5

Nombre _____

Hora _____

Fecha _____

EPISODIO 5

Para pensar

At the end of this episode, Rosalinda tells Lola *"Las amigas de Carmela son amigas mías."*
What does she mean? Are your friends' friends also your friends? Why or why not? What is a
good friend? Discuss this concept with other students.

Para observar

Listen for a Spanish verb form and pronoun that are only used in Spain. See if you can count
how many times they're used.

In English you say "OK" to indicate your approval. Try to catch the Spanish equivalent that
Lola uses in the video.

Listen for the title of the video toward the end of the episode.

Después de ver el video

¿Qué observas?

1. What are the pronoun and verb form that are only used in Spain and that are spoken in the video? _____

2. What Spanish word is similar to "OK"? _____

3. Who says the title of the video and what does she mean?

_____

¿Comprendes?

A. Draw a line from each quotation from the video to the scene it corresponds to.

1. "¿Eres tú, María?"
2. "Ni un papel. Nada, absolutamente nada sobre María Requena."
3. "Primero, quiero hablar de una paciente que se llama María Requena."

© Pearson Education, Inc. All rights reserved.

Realidades 1

Nombre _____

Hora _____

Episodio 5

Fecha _____

EPISODIO 5

B. Write the name of the character who matches each description.

1. Es una amiga de Carmela. _Rosalinda_

2. Es la mejor amiga de Lola. _Carmela_

3. Es la abuela de Pedro Requena. _Doña Gracia_

4. Es el nieto de doña Gracia. _Pedro_

5. Es la sobrina de doña Gracia. _María_

C. Circle the letter (A or B) of the phrase that best describes each scene.

1.

A. Rosalinda sabe algo del accidente de coches de las dos chicas.
B. Rosalinda tiene mucha información en los archivos de las chicas.

2.

A. Lola descubre que Julia murió en el accidente.
B. Lola descubre que María murió en el accidente.

3.

A. Doña Gracia sabe que María está en el hospital.
B. Doña Gracia quiere hablar con María.

© Pearson Education, Inc. All rights reserved.

Realidades ❶

Episodio 5

Nombre _____

Fecha _____

Hora _____

EPISODIO 5

D. Write the number of the phrase that best describes each scene on the appropriate line.

___1___   ___4___   ___3___   ___2___

1. Lola y Carmela van a verle a Rosalinda en el hospital.

2. Rosalinda les dice que no hay nada sobre las chicas.

3. Rosalinda es amiga de Carmela.

4. Doña Gracia pregunta si ella es María.

 Para hablar

You and a partner are going to replay the conversation between Lola and Rosalinda. Use an empty file folder to add more drama to the scene. Practice and then prepare to perform it in front of the class.

Lola:

• Ask Rosalinda if she remembers María Requena.

• Ask what happened to her.

• Tell her you want more information.

• Thank her for her help and say goodbye.

Rosalinda:

• Say yes, you remember María Requena.

• Say that she was in a car accident.

• Tell her there's nothing in the hospital records.

• Tell her you're sorry and then goodbye.

© Pearson Education, Inc. All rights reserved.

Realidades ❶

Episodio 5

Nombre _____

Fecha _____

Hora _____

EPISODIO 5

Para decir más

Estuvo en un accidente. She was in an accident.
No hay absolutamente nada sobre There is absolutely nothing about
  María Requena. María Requena.
¿Qué le pasó a ella? What happened to her?
¿Te acuerdas de María Requena? Do you remember María Requena?

Para escribir

Help Lola with her notes about this case. Make a list of what she has learned so far about doña Gracia and María Requena. Include three or four sentences to describe each one.

You might start with:
María Requena es la sobrina de doña Gracia. Es alta y muy guapa . . .

_____
_____
_____
_____
_____
_____
_____
_____
_____
_____
_____

© Pearson Education, Inc. All rights reserved.

Realidades ❶

Episodio 5

Nombre _____

Fecha _____

Hora _____

EPISODIO 5

Nota cultural

La amistad

Lola and Carmela are very good friends, and so are Carmela and Rosalinda. Friendship (*La amistad*) is not taken lightly in the Spanish-speaking world. *Un amigo* or *una amiga* is usually a friend for life. These friends spend free time with each other and get to know each other's families. Close friends, rather like extended family, are often included in family events and celebrations. While Spanish speakers are cordial to people they don't know very well—*conocidos,* or acquaintances—these people are not yet *amigos.* Nor are classmates (*compañeros de clase*) or coworkers (*compañeros de trabajo*) *amigos,* even though all might get along very well. It takes time to forge a friendship.

From what you've seen of the video so far, which of the characters do you think are: *¿Amigos o amigas? ¿Compañeros de trabajo? ¿Conocidos? ¿Familia?* Work with four or five other students to make a chart that shows these categories. Then, write the appropriate characters' names under each heading. Be sure to include as many pairs of characters as you can. Share your ideas with the rest of the class.

© Pearson Education, Inc. All rights reserved.

Realidades ❶

Episodio 5

Nombre _____

Fecha _____

Hora _____

EPISODIO 5

Nota cultural

Saludos

In *Episodio* 4 Lola greets Carmela with a light kiss on both cheeks. In this *Episodio* Carmela greets Rosalinda the same way. This is a common greeting between girl-friends. When people greet one another, there is usually some physical contact as well as verbal exchange. Friends and acquaintances almost always shake hands when meeting and departing. Women often embrace and kiss on one or both cheeks. Often, only their cheeks touch; the kiss is more of a gesture than a real kiss. Men and women may also embrace and kiss on the cheek, but this is usually reserved for relatives or close friends. Men often embrace, especially if they haven't seen each other for a while.

How do you greet your friends of the same sex? of the opposite sex? _____

_____

_____

_____

How do you greet close family members? more distant relatives? _____

_____

_____

_____

Para explorar en Internet

Go online to locate a free greeting card service. Make and then send a friendship card to someone special. Remember to write your greeting in Spanish.

© Pearson Education, Inc. All rights reserved.

Realidades ❶

Episodio 6

Nombre _____

Fecha _____

Hora _____

EPISODIO 6

Antes de ver el video

Resumen del episodio

Lola llega a su oficina y hay un recado de Pedro Requena. Él viene a hablar con ella sobre su abuela, doña Gracia. Necesita a un detective privado y quiere la ayuda de Lola. Pedro explica que su abuela es una mujer muy rica y que tiene unas joyas preciosas. Pero hay un problema. Las joyas de doña Gracia no están en el piso. Pedro cree que un ladrón robó las joyas. Pero, ¿cómo sabe el ladrón que hay joyas en el piso de doña Gracia?

Vocabulario

una cita   an appointment
un recado   a message

Frases importantes

Acabo de venir del hospital.   I just came from the hospital.
El ladrón robó . . .   The robber stole . . .
Necesito saber . . .   I need to know . . .
Nosotros cobramos . . .   We charge . . .
Vi a su abuela.   I saw your grandmother.

Para pensar

Lola says that for her, *"la investigación es como un deporte."* What does she mean by this? How does this tell you that she enjoys her job? Do you think most people would say this about their chosen profession? Discuss this with other students.

Para observar

There are several ways to say goodbye in Spanish. Listen for four of these expressions at the end of the *Episodio*.

© Pearson Education, Inc. All rights reserved.

Realidades ①

Episodio 6

Nombre _____

Fecha _____

Hora _____

EPISODIO 6

Después de ver el video

¿Qué observas?

What expressions are used in this *Episodio* to say goodbye? How do you usually say goodbye to your friends? to your teachers? to your parents' friends? _____

_____

¿Comprendes?

A. Circle the letter (A or B) of the phrase that best corresponds to each scene from the video.

1.

   Ⓐ Margarita tiene un recado para Lola.
   B. Lola tiene un recado para Margarita.

2.

   Ⓐ Pedro dice que su abuela tiene muchas joyas.
   B. Pedro dice que su abuela tiene muchos coches.

3.

   A. Pedro tiene un nuevo cliente.
   Ⓑ Lola tiene un nuevo cliente.

© Pearson Education, Inc. All rights reserved.

4.

a. Margarita trabaja mucho.

b. Margarita habla mucho por teléfono.

c. Margarita escribe mucho.

5.

a. Lola está feliz porque no hay más clientes.

b. Lola está feliz porque hay un cliente nuevo.

c. Lola está feliz porque no hay más dinero.

6.

a. Margarita tiene una cita con Lola.

b. Pedro tiene un recado para Lola.

c. Pedro tiene una cita con Lola.

7.

a. Pedro quiere la ayuda de Lola.

b. Pedro quiere comer con Lola.

c. Pedro tiene un recado para Margarita.

© Pearson Education, Inc. All rights reserved.

B. Write the word that best completes each quotation from the video. Then, write the name of the character who said it.

1. "Creo que tengo un nuevo _____". _Lola_ ✓
   - a. dinero
   - ✓ b. deporte
   - (c.) cliente
   - d. recado

2. "Por fin, un cliente con _____". _Paco_ ✓
   - a. cita
   - ✓ (b.) dinero
   - c. segundo
   - d. raro

3. "Pedro, acabo de venir del _____". _Lola_ ✓
   - a. hotel
   - ✓ b. colegio
   - (c.) oficina
   - d. hospital

4. "Para mí la investigación es como un _____". _lola_
   - a. cliente
   - ✓ (b.) deporte
   - c. periódico
   - d. piso

5. "Mi abuela tiene dinero y unas _____". _pacdo_ ✓
   - a. sobrinas
   - ✓ b. nietas
   - (c.) joyas
   - d. revistas

© Pearson Education, Inc. All rights reserved.

C. Read each sentence and write *C* (*cierto*) if it is true and *F* (*falso*) if it is false. If it is false, rewrite the necessary information to make it true.

1. Pedro quiere una investigadora. _____

2. Margarita trabaja mucho en la oficina de Lola y Paco. _____
   _____

3. Las joyas están en el piso. _____

4. La abuela, doña Gracia, está en el Hotel San Carlos. _____
   _____

5. El ladrón robó solamente dinero. _____

6. Lola y Paco van a buscar las joyas. _____

7. Pedro va a recibir todo de su abuela. _____

8. Paco es el nieto de doña Gracia. _____
   _____

9. El ladrón sabe mucho acerca de doña Gracia. _____

D. Circle the letter of the word that best completes each sentence.

1. Margarita _____ mucho por teléfono.
   a. trabaja   b. escribe   c. habla

2. Paco _____ con Lola.
   a. trabaja   b. lee   c. nada

3. Pedro tiene una cita con Lola a _____.
   a. las dos   b. las seis y media   c. la una y media

4. Pedro es el _____ de doña Gracia.
   a. nieto   b. sobrino   c. tío

5. Doña Gracia es una mujer _____.
   a. pobre   b. rica   c. joven

6. El ladrón sabe que hay _____ en el piso.
   a. comida   b. periódicos   c. joyas

7. Pedro quiere _____.
   a. un detective privado   b. un inspector   c. un policía

© Pearson Education, Inc. All rights reserved.

Realidades 1

Episodio 6

Nombre _____

Hora _____

Fecha _____

EPISODIO 6

 Para hablar

Margarita needs some help to become a better secretary. You and your partner are Margarita and Lola. First Margarita gives Lola *un recado* and later tells her *su cita* has arrived. You might want to use a small piece of paper to represent the message.

Margarita:
- Greet Lola and ask how she is.
- Give her a message.
- Tell her that her *cita* has arrived.

Lola:
- Respond to Margarita's greeting.
- Thank her for the message and read it.
- Greet your appointment and show him or her to your office.

> **Para decir más**
>
> **está aquí**   he's here
> **para ti**   for you

 Para escribir

Paco is thrilled that Lola has a new client, but he needs some information so he can help her. Write up the case for Paco, including a description of Pedro, María, and doña Gracia.

You might start with:

María va a recibir toda la fortuna de su tía, doña Gracia.
Pedro vive en Italia . . .

© Pearson Education, Inc. All rights reserved.

Realidades ❶

Episodio 6

Nombre _____

Fecha _____

Hora _____

EPISODIO 6

Nota cultural

Tutear

In this *episodio*, Pedro says to Lola: *"Por favor, ¿por qué no me tuteas?"* He is giving Lola permission to use the *tú* form of verbs in conversation with him. He is acknowledging her as a peer or an equal. He doesn't want her to use the more formal *usted* in their dealings. Lola is right to greet him with *usted* until he asks her to address him with *tú*.

The use of *tú* is called *el tuteo*; to use *tú* with someone is *tutear*. *Tú* is used in informal address with friends, classmates, and family (including pets). *Tú* creates an atmosphere of closeness; *usted* creates some distance.

If *usted* is expected and *tú* is used, it could be considered an insult, a way of putting someone down. Because of the cultural shock for Spanish speakers who hear *tú* when *usted* should be used, if you have the slightest doubt whether to use *tú* or *usted* you should use *usted*. If the person wishes you to use *tú*, he or she will quickly indicate that. This is exactly what Pedro does when he tells Lola, *"Por favor, ¿por qué no me tuteas?"*

Based on what you know about the uses of *tú* and *usted,* how would you address the following people?

1. tu hermanita _____

2. tu profesora _____

3. el Presidente de los Estados

   Unidos _____

4. la madre de una amiga _____

5. tu abuelo _____

6. una amiga de tus padres _____

7. tu vecino de 70 años _____

8. tu primo de 20 años _____

9. una camarera _____

10. tu perro _____

Now, how do these characters address each other, with *tú* or *usted*?

1. doña Lupe y Lola _____

2. Lola y Carmela _____

3. Carmela y Rosalinda _____

4. el Inspector Gil y doña Lupe

   _____

5. Margarita y Lola _____

© Pearson Education, Inc. All rights reserved.

Realidades ❶

Nombre _____

Hora _____

Episodio 6

Fecha _____

EPISODIO 6

Nota cultural

Euros

Euros are mentioned again in this *Episodio* when Lola tells Pedro, *"Nosotros cobramos 150 euros más los gastos."* Euros are used as the monetary exchange in 12 of the 15 European Union countries: Austria, Belgium, Finland, France, Germany, Greece, Holland, Ireland, Italy, Luxembourg, Portugal, and Spain. The seven bank notes (in denominations of 5, 10, 20, 50, 100, 200, and 500 euros) are in different colors and sizes with designs that are symbolic of Europe's architectural heritage. The front of the notes show windows and gateways, which symbolize the spirit of openness and cooperation in the European Union. The reverse side of each note features a bridge from a particular age, a metaphor for communication between the people of Europe and the rest of the world. The euro was first used on January 1, 2002, and the *peseta*, the former currency of Spain, was accepted for two months and then replaced by the euro.

What is the euro and when was it first used?

_____

What countries use the euro as their currency? _____

_____

_____

What are the denominations of the euro bills? _____

What was the former currency of Spain? _____

© Pearson Education, Inc. All rights reserved.

Realidades 1

Episodio 6

Nombre _____

Fecha _____

Hora _____

EPISODIO 6

Para explorar en Internet

Go online to find more information about the euro, as well as the history of the former currency in Spain, *la peseta*. Write up your findings.

© Pearson Education, Inc. All rights reserved.

Realidades ❶

Episodio 7

Nombre _____

Fecha _____

Hora _____

EPISODIO 7

Antes de ver el video

Resumen del episodio

Lola y Pedro visitan el piso elegante de doña Gracia. Entran en el dormitorio de María. Allí encuentran[1] una foto y una tarjeta postal de Barcelona. Después van al piso de Julia. Allí vive un joven que no conoce a Julia, pero dice que[2] antes vivía[3] una chica en el piso. Todavía hay unas cosas de esa chica: unas cartas y unos papeles. ¿Y quién escribe estas cartas?

[1] find   [2] says that   [3] used to live

Vocabulario

¡Qué casualidad!   What a coincidence!
¡Suerte!   Good luck!

Frases importantes

No la conozco.   I don't know her.
Tenía un secretario.   He had a secretary.
Tuvo problemas con él.   He had problems with him.

Para pensar

Lola says that *"la casualidad no existe."* What do you think? Do you believe in coincidence or chance? What role has coincidence or chance ever played in your life? Discuss this with other students.

Para observar

Pay attention to how Lola and Pedro get to Julia's building and how they get in.

Después de ver el video

¿Qué observas?

1. ¿Qué transporte usan Lola y Pedro para ir al piso de Julia? __taxi__

2. Lola usa llaves para entrar en el edificio de Julia. ¿Por qué las tiene? _____
   _She found the keys at the ... _

© Pearson Education, Inc. All rights reserved.

Realidades 1

Episodio 7

Nombre _____

Fecha _____

Hora _____

EPISODIO 7

¿Comprendes?

A. Write an X next to each item you saw in María's room.

1. _____ una lámpara
2. _____ un televisor
3. _____ una mesa
4. _____ unos papeles
5. _____ una foto
6. _____ una cama
7. _____ una silla
8. _____ unos libros

B. Write the letter of the scene from the video that best corresponds to each description.

a.  b.  c.  d.

e.

_____ **1.** Rosalinda llama con la dirección de Julia.

_____ **2.** Lola y Pedro van al piso de Julia.

_____ **3.** Pedro pregunta si Lola quiere visitar el piso de su abuela.

_____ **4.** Pedro y Lola miran unas cartas de Julia.

_____ **5.** Pedro y Lola miran la tarjeta postal de Barcelona.

© Pearson Education, Inc. All rights reserved.

C. Write the word from the box that best completes each sentence.

En este episodio, Lola recibe una ___llamada___ de Rosalinda. Luego ella va con

Pedro para ver el ___dormitorio___ ✓ de María. Allí, miran una ___tarjeta postal___ ✓

de Barcelona. Después van al ___piso___ ✓ de Julia. Ella no está allí, pero un

joven les da ___cartas___ ✓ para ella de Luis Antonio. Pedro y Lola piensan que

hay muchas ___casualidades___ ✓.

casualidades	detective
llamada	dormitorio
piso	cartas
tarjeta postal	taxi

D. Put these scenes from the video in the order in which they occured by writing *1* under the first scene and *4* under the last scene. Then, write a brief description of each scene in Spanish.

4 _____

1 _____

© Pearson Education, Inc. All rights reserved.

Realidades ❶

Episodio 7

Nombre _____

Fecha _____

Hora _____

EPISODIO 7

2 _____

5 _____

E. In each group of sentences below there are two true sentences and one false sentence. Circle the letter of the false sentence in each group.

1. **a.** Rosalinda es una amiga de Carmela.
   b. Carmela es una amiga de Lola.
   c. Rosalinda es una amiga de Lola.

2. **a.** Pedro llama a Lola por teléfono.
   b. María llama a Lola por teléfono.
   c. Rosalinda llama a Lola por teléfono.

3. **a.** Lola y Pedro van a la casa de doña Gracia.
   b. Lola y Pedro van al piso de Julia.
   c. Lola y Pedro van a la casa de doña Lupe.

4. **a.** Lola dice que en su profesión la casualidad no existe.
   b. Lola dice que hay un taxi en la calle.
   c. Pedro dice que Luis Antonio y su hijo viven en Barcelona.

5. **a.** Luis Antonio es uno de los enfermeros del hospital.
   b. Luis Antonio ayudó a las dos chicas.
   c. Luis Antonio es uno de los doctores del hospital.

© Pearson Education, Inc. All rights reserved.

Para hablar

Work with a partner to role-play a phone call in which you ask for the phone number and address of a friend. Sit back to back for a more realistic conversation. That way you cannot use gestures to communicate your meaning. Remember to answer the phone with *Diga* or *Dígame,* as people do in Spain.

Estudiante A:

- Answer the phone.

- Answer your partner's question and ask how he or she is.

- Give your partner the information.

- Give your partner the address. Remember to add a floor number and apartment identification.

- Say you're welcome and goodbye.

Estudiante B:

- Say hello and ask how your partner is.

- Answer and then ask for the phone number of someone you both know.

- Now ask for the address of the same person.

- Thank your partner for the information.

- Say you'll see your partner later.

 Para escribir

Make a wanted poster *(se busca)* for the thief who took doña Gracia's jewels. Include what you know—or think you know—about him or her, the date on which the jewels were taken, and a description (or an illustration) of the missing jewelry. Use some of the following words to write your description.

© Pearson Education, Inc. All rights reserved.

Realidades ❶

Episodio 7

Nombre _____

Fecha _____

Hora _____

EPISODIO 7

Para decir más

buscamos   we're looking for
el collar de perlas   pearl necklace
desaparecer   to disappear
los diamantes   diamonds
entrar en   to enter (in)
las esmeraldas   emeralds
el ladrón, la ladrona   thief
la recompensa   reward

Nota cultural

Las direcciones

The items in an address in Spain are written in this order: indication of whether it is a street, avenue, boulevard, etc.; street name; street number; floor number; and apartment letter or number. In urban areas, each floor of a high-rise apartment building may have only one or two large apartments. Generally, the numbers in street addresses are low; it is not common to have four- or five-digit numbers. This is because buildings are numbered in sequence along a street, not the way it is done in many places in the United States.

The address for Julia is: calle Norte, 23, 1°, D. That means she lives on Norte Street, number 23, on the first floor, and in apartment D. If there are only two apartments to a floor, sometimes they are indicated by *dcha.* (for *derecha*, or "right") or *izq.* or *izqda.* (for *izquierda*, or "left").

Write your address in the Spanish style. If you don't live in an apartment building, make up an imaginary floor and apartment number.

_____

© Pearson Education, Inc. All rights reserved.

Realidades ①

Episodio 7

Nombre _____

Fecha _____

Hora _____

EPISODIO 7

Nota cultural

Barcelona

The postcard Lola and Pedro find in María's room shows the *Templo de la Sagrada Familia*, perhaps the most famous landmark in Barcelona. Located in northeastern Spain, and on the Mediterranean Sea, Barcelona is the second largest city in Spain, the capital of the autonomous community of Cataluña, and the country's major commercial and industrial center. It has been an important seaport for more than a thousand years. In addition to speaking Spanish, the people of this region also speak *catalán*, one of Spain's four official languages. Barcelona was the site of the 1992 Summer Olympics.

One of the greatest architects of Barcelona—and of Spain—was Antonio Gaudí. The construction of the famous *Templo de la Sagrada Familia* was begun in 1882, and Gaudí took charge of the project shortly thereafter. From then until his death in 1926, Gaudí oversaw the construction of this ambitious temple that is still unfinished. Gaudí's work can be seen in many other public and private buildings in Barcelona. One very popular spot is the *Parque Güell*, a city park since 1922. A dragon made of mosaics greets visitors at the entrance.

What is the most famous landmark in your city or town? _____

_____

_____

_____

Why is it important? _____

_____

_____

_____

© Pearson Education, Inc. All rights reserved.

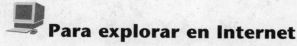

Realidades 1

Episodio 7

Nombre _____

Hora _____

Fecha _____

EPISODIO 7

Para explorar en Internet

Go online to research either *La Sagrada Familia* (you might try to find out more about the current push to finish the building) or the Spanish architect Antonio Gaudí and some of his other landmark designs. Write up your findings.

© Pearson Education, Inc. All rights reserved.

Antes de ver el video

Resumen del episodio

Después de visitar el piso de Julia, Lola y Pedro van a un café para tomar algo. Hablan de las cosas de Julia que el joven acaba de darles.[1] Cuando Lola llega a su piso por la noche, ve que una mujer entra en el edificio número 8. Lola cree que es María y sale[2] rápidamente de su piso y espera[3] enfrente. Luego la mujer sale del edificio y Lola le pregunta, "Eres tú, María?"

[1] just gave them   [2] she leaves   [3] she waits

Personajes

¿Eres tú, María?

Vocabulario

Acabo de hablar con . . .   I just spoke with . . .
Acabo de ver . . .   I just saw . . .
muerta   dead

Frases importantes

Ella las perdió.   She lost them.
María tenía las llaves.   María had the keys.
¡No me sigas!   Don't follow me!

Para pensar

In this *Episodio*, Lola asks a young woman if she is María. How would you react if a stranger approached you at night and asked you your name? Would you talk to the stranger and answer the question, or leave the situation as quickly as possible? Discuss what you would do and why with other students.

© Pearson Education, Inc. All rights reserved.

Realidades ①

Episodio 8

Nombre _____

Fecha _____

Hora _____

EPISODIO 8

Para observar

Sometimes you don't need to wear a watch to know what time it is when you're not home. Pay attention to how Lola knows what time it is and how long she waits.

Después de ver el video

¿Qué observas?

¿A qué mira Lola para saber la hora? ¿Cuánto tiempo espera a María?

_____

_____

¿Comprendes?

A. Write the letter of each scene of the video next to the quotation it corresponds to.

a.

b.

c.

d.

_____ **1.** "Las diez y media. ¡Ay! Por fin . . ."

_____ **2.** "Oye, hay algo que no comprendo. ¿Cómo es que tienes las llaves del piso de Julia?"

_____ **3.** "¿Raro? ¿Por qué? Las joyas de doña Gracia no están en el piso. María robó las joyas y ya está."

_____ **4.** "¿Eres tú, María?"

© Pearson Education, Inc. All rights reserved.

Realidades ①

Episodio 8

Nombre _____

Fecha _____

Hora _____

EPISODIO 8

B. Answer the following questions in complete sentences. Use the scenes from the video to help you.

1. ¿Dónde están Lola y Pedro? ¿Qué hacen?

   _____

   _____

2. Según el Inspector Gil, ¿quién robó las joyas?

   _____

   _____

3. ¿Dónde espera Lola? _____

   _____

4. ¿Qué tienen Pedro y Lola de Julia? _____

   _____

© Pearson Education, Inc. All rights reserved.

Realidades ❶

Episodio 8

Nombre _____

Hora _____

Fecha _____

EPISODIO 8

5. ¿Qué pregunta Lola a la mujer? _____

_____

C. Circle the letter of the word or words that best complete each sentence.

1. En el café Lola toma _____.
   a. leche
   b. café
   c. agua con gas
   d. un refresco

2. Julia está en la foto con _____.
   a. Carmela
   b. Rosalinda
   c. un hombre
   d. su tía

3. Lola usa _____ de María para entrar en el edificio de Julia.
   a. los papeles
   b. las tarjetas
   c. las llaves
   d. las llamadas

4. Lola dice que acaba de ver _____.
   a. al Inspector Gil
   b. al Inspector Peña
   c. a Carmela
   d. a María Requena

5. El Inspector Gil piensa que _____ robó las joyas de doña Gracia.
   a. Julia
   b. María
   c. doña Lupe
   d. Pedro

© Pearson Education, Inc. All rights reserved.

Realidades 1

Nombre

Hora

Episodio 8

Fecha

EPISODIO 8

6. María le dice a Lola: _____
   a. ¡No me sigas!
   b. Diga.
   c. Sí, yo quiero.
   d. ¿No cree?

7. _____ va a recibir todo de doña Gracia.
   a. María
   b. Pedro
   c. Doña Lupe
   d. Julia

8. Lola dice que todo esto es _____.
   a. interesante
   b. muy lógico
   c. fantástico
   d. un poco raro

9. Lola habló con María delante _____.
   a. del piso de doña Gracia
   b. del hospital
   c. del piso de Pedro
   d. de la casa de Rosalinda

10. _____ tenía las llaves del piso de Julia.
    a. Pedro
    b. Carmela
    c. María
    d. El Inspector Peña

© Pearson Education, Inc. All rights reserved.

Realidades ❶

Episodio 8

Nombre _____

Fecha _____

Hora _____

EPISODIO 8

 **Para hablar**

Work with a partner to role-play the conversation between Lola and Inspector Gil. You may base your conversation on what is really said in the video, or create something completely new. An example follows.

Inspector Gil:

- Dígame.

- ¿Cómo? ¿Dónde hablaste con ella?

- Estamos buscándola. María es la ladrona que robó las joyas.

- Ud. sabe mucho, ¡pero esto es cosa de la policía!

- Qué interesante. Pero no olvide decirle todo a la policía.

Lola:

- Buenas noches, Inspector Gil. Soy Lola Lago y acabo de hablar con María Requena.

- Hablamos delante del piso de su tía, doña Gracia.

- Pero María va a recibir todo de doña Gracia. ¿Por qué necesita robar las joyas?

- Sí, yo lo sé, pero es también mi caso. Ahora trabajo para Pedro Requena, el nieto de doña Gracia.

- Claro. Adiós.

Para decir más

acabo de hablar / ver   I just spoke /saw
estamos buscándola   we're looking for her
es mi caso   it's my case
es raro   it's strange
lo sé   I know

© Pearson Education, Inc. All rights reserved.

Realidades ❶

Episodio 8

Nombre _____

Fecha _____

Hora _____

EPISODIO 8

Para escribir

Look at this scene from the video. Write five sentences to describe the scene and the conversation between Lola and Pedro.

_____

_____

_____

_____

_____

Nota cultural

¡Dios mío!

At the beginning of this episode María says *¡Dios mío!* (My God!) to express her frustration. Doña Lupe also uses this expression as well as *¡Por Dios!* in earlier episodes. Spaniards often punctuate their speech with expressions using *Dios* and *Jesús*, which are acceptable in Spanish. For example, when someone sneezes, you may say *Salud* or *Jesús*.

What other expressions that show frustration or shock do you recall from the video?

_____

_____

© Pearson Education, Inc. All rights reserved.

Realidades ❶

Episodio 8

Nombre _____

Fecha _____

Hora _____

EPISODIO 8

Nota cultural

La hora de cenar

Lola calls Inspector Gil around 10:30 P.M. Even though the police keep hours around the clock, in Spain 10:30 would not be considered very late even to call a friend. Spaniards usually have dinner between 9:00 and 10:00 if they're eating at home, and it is not uncommon to make a dinner reservation for 11:00 P.M. Breakfast is a light meal: a warm drink, plus bread or a sweet roll. *Tapas* (or *la hora del aperitivo*) precedes lunch, which is usually served between 2:00 and 3:00 in the afternoon. Around 6:00, people enjoy *la merienda*, a snack of tea, coffee, or hot chocolate plus as assortment of pastries, breads, or little sandwiches. Before dinner, friends might go out for a round of *tapas*.

How do the Spanish mealtimes and eating habits differ from yours? What similarities are there? Which schedule do you prefer? Why?

_____

_____

_____

_____

_____

_____

© Pearson Education, Inc. All rights reserved.

Realidades 1

Episodio 8

Nombre

Fecha

Hora

EPISODIO 8

Para explorar en Internet

Go online to learn more about Madrid and Barcelona. Based on what you know of the two cities, where would you prefer to live? Why?

_____

_____

_____

_____

_____

_____

_____

© Pearson Education, Inc. All rights reserved.

Realidades ①

Episodio 9

Nombre _____

Fecha _____

Hora _____

EPISODIO 9

Antes de ver el video

Resumen del episodio

Al día siguiente Lola va a su trabajo, cuando ve a María. ¡Qué suerte! Lola la sigue[1] y llama a Paco y a Margarita. Ella necesita a los dos ahora mismo para ayudarla. Vigilan[2] a María y a un hombre en el café, y Margarita muestra[3] sus talentos de detective. Es evidente que María y el hombre no están nada contentos. Pero, ¿quién es este hombre misterioso y por qué quiere irse de Madrid?

[1] follows   [2] They watch   [3] shows

Personajes

¿Quiénes son? ¿De qué están hablando?

Vocabulario

aparece   appears
ve a sentarte   go sit
¡Venid!   Come!

Frases importantes

Basta de detective por hoy.   That's it for being a detective today.
¿Estás segura?   Are you sure?
quiere irse   he wants to go away
Tengo que colgar.   I have to hang up.
vengan en seguida   come right away

Para pensar

In this episode, Margarita tries her hand at playing detective. Based on what you know about her, how do you think she'll do? Does she have any qualities a good detective should have? Discuss this with other students.

© Pearson Education, Inc. All rights reserved.

Realidades ①

Episodio 9

Nombre _____

Fecha _____

Hora _____

EPISODIO 9

Para observar

Observe Lola's surroundings as she follows María through Madrid.

Después de ver el video

¿Qué observas?

¿Qué lugares (places), personas o cosas pasa Lola mientras sigue a María por Madrid?

_____

_____

_____

¿Comprendes?

A. Match each scene from the video with its description by writing the appropriate letter on the blank.

1.  _____

2.  _____

3.  _____

4.  _____

© Pearson Education, Inc. All rights reserved.

Realidades ①

Episodio 9

Nombre _____

Fecha _____

Hora _____

EPISODIO 9

5. _____

a. Lola les explica el problema.
b. María espera a Luis Antonio.
c. Lola sigue a María.
d. María y Luis Antonio hablan en el café.
e. Margarita escucha todo.

B. Look at the scenes from the video and write a brief description of each one.

1.

_____

2. ![escena]

_____

3. ![escena]

_____

_____

© Pearson Education, Inc. All rights reserved.

Realidades ❶

Episodio 9

Nombre _____

Fecha _____

Hora _____

EPISODIO 9

4.

_____

_____

5.

_____

_____

C. Who said each quotation from the video below?

1. "¿De parte de quién?" _____

2. "Te necesito ahora mismo. Y Margarita también." _____

3. "Yo quiero ser detective. Yo quiero ir allí." _____

4. "Él dice que quiere irse de Madrid." _____

5. "¿Julia? ¿Estás segura?" _____

6. "Pero, oye, oye . . ." _____

7. "Estoy en la Estación de Chamartín." _____

8. "Le vuelvo a llamar más tarde." _____

9. "Yo ayudé mucho." _____

10. "Va a ir en tren. Andén 1." _____

© Pearson Education, Inc. All rights reserved.

Realidades ➊

Episodio 9

Nombre _____

Fecha _____

Hora _____

EPISODIO 9

 Para hablar

Some Spaniards have a coat of arms that represents their family. Work with a partner to make a coat of arms *(un escudo)* for one of the characters in *¿Eres tú, María?* First, make a list of any four of the following categories: *le gusta(n), no le gusta(n), profesión, familia, descripción, lo que hace en el misterio.* Under each category, write (in Spanish) what you remember about the character. If certain information doesn't appear in the video, make it up! Make a sketch of *el escudo* and divide it into four sections, one for each of the categories you chose. Based on the information from each of your categories, draw something symbolic for each section. You can also use illustrations from magazines or download pictures from the Internet. Work with your partner to explain who your character is, the categories you chose, and what the illustrations represent. Then, present your *escudo* to the rest of the class.

You might start by saying:

La persona del escudo es doña Gracia. Aquí hay una ilustración de joyas, porque doña Gracia es muy rica y tiene muchas joyas. Aquí está su casa. Es muy elegante . . .

 Para escribir

A Lola le gustan muchas cosas: su trabajo, leer el periódico, caminar, el café con leche, los churros, las plantas, los secretos y caminar. Y también es trabajadora y sociable.

Do you share many traits or interests with Lola? Make a Venn diagram: two intertwining circles. In the left circle list Lola's qualities, traits, and interests. In the right circle, describe yourself. Then, in the intersecting area, write what the two of you have in common. For example, you both might be hardworking, so you'd include *trabajador(a)* there.

Now write three short paragraphs about yourself and Lola, describing your similarities and differences. The first paragraph describes Lola, the second one describes you, and the third compares the two of you. For example, your first paragraph might begin:

Lola es alta y con el pelo corto y moreno. Le gustan . . .

The second paragraph might begin:

Yo soy rubia con ojos azules . . .

In the third paragraph you might write:

Lola y yo somos similares y diferentes. Nos gustan los secretos y las plantas, pero no me gusta . . .

Include at least three sentences in each paragraph. Exchange your paper with a partner before turning it in or sharing it with the rest of the class. Proofreading each other's work often helps catch mistakes in spelling, word choice, and verb tense. Careful proofreading can lead to a better paper.

© Pearson Education, Inc. All rights reserved.

Realidades ❶

Episodio 9

Nombre _____

Hora _____

Fecha _____

EPISODIO 9

Nota cultural

Los cupones

At the beginning of the video you hear and see a man selling some "papers" on the street. The papers are daily lottery tickets, and they are sold by the visually impaired. The winnings for this kind of lottery *(cupones pro-ciegos)* are not in the millions, but the tickets do offer a variety of cash prizes and are extremely popular. They have been around for more than 65 years. A non-profit organization, ONCE *(Organización Nacional de Ciegos Españoles)* has been sponsoring *los cupones* since 1938; funds channeled through ONCE go to the improvement of services for the visually impaired.

Can you think of anything in your experience that is similar to *los cupones*?

_____

_____

_____

© Pearson Education, Inc. All rights reserved.

Realidades 1

Episodio 9

Nombre _____

Fecha _____

Hora _____

EPISODIO 9

Nota cultural

El metro

Public transportation in Madrid is very accessible, and the subway *(el metro)* is clean, cheap, and very fast. Because Madrid is an old city with many narrow and congested streets, *el metro* is the transportation of choice: there are no traffic jams below the streets of the capital! This rapid means of transit has 12 color-coded lines, which add up to more than 170 kilometers of line and more than 150 stations. The service operates between 6 A.M. and 1:30 A.M. every day of the year. A one-way or single ticket *(un billete sencillo)* is available for a little more than $1, and a ticket for 10 rides is even cheaper per ride. With a single ticket, a rider may transfer any number of times without leaving the metro confines. *El metro* now goes as far as the airport. Monthly and even yearly passes are available and special rates for children and senior citizens apply.

¿Hay un metro en tu ciudad, o en una ciudad cerca de tu ciudad? ¿Cómo es?

_____

_____

_____

Para explorar en Internet

Go online to find out more about ONCE and how the look of *los cupones* has evolved. Find a sample *cupón* to learn how the prize monies are distributed. Write up your findings.

© Pearson Education, Inc. All rights reserved.

Realidades 1

Episodio 10

Nombre _____

Fecha _____

Hora _____

EPISODIO 10

Antes de ver el video

Resumen del episodio

Es el último episodio y Lola soluciona todo. Vas a descubrir[1] quién es María. Vas a saber por qué Luis Antonio quiere irse de Madrid. ¿Quién tiene las joyas? ¿Cómo y por qué ocurrió el crimen? ¿Quién va a la cárcel?[2] ¿Quién va a necesitar un buen abogado?[3] ¿Va a conocer Pedro a su abuela por fin?

[1]discover [2]jail [3]lawyer

Vocabulario

atacar   to attack
listos   ready
mucha suerte   a lot of luck
no quiere esperar   (he) doesn't want to wait
los novios   boyfriend and girlfriend
las reconoció   (he) recognized them
robarlas   to steal them
tomó   (she) took

Frases importantes

Deténgala.   Arrest her.
Él pierde la paciencia.   He loses his patience.
Eso parece.   That's what it seems like.
No quería.   I didn't want to.

Para pensar

Based on what you know from watching *¿Eres tú, María?*, who do you think took doña Gracia's jewels? Why do you think this person is the thief? Who do you think is completely innocent of this crime? Why? Discuss your ideas with other students.

Para observar

In *Episodio 7* Lola said that *"la casualidad no existe,"* yet Inspector Gil says *"¡Qué casualidad!"* when talking about the case. Think about all the coincidences as you watch the last *Episodio* of *¿Eres tú, María?*

© Pearson Education, Inc. All rights reserved.

Realidades ❶

Episodio 10

Nombre _____

Fecha _____

Hora _____

EPISODIO 10

Después de ver el video

¿Qué observas?

¿Qué casualidades hay en el video? Menciona por lo menos cuatro.

_____

_____

_____

_____

¿Comprendes?

A. Look at each scene from the video below. Then, circle the letter of the sentence that best describes what is happening.

1.

   a. Pedro y Lola van a Barcelona.

   b. Pedro y Lola van a cenar.

2.

   a. Lola explica que Julia tomó la identidad de María.

   b. Lola explica que Julia robó las joyas.

3.

   a. Julia y Luis Antonio son hermanos.

   b. Julia y Luis Antonio son novios.

© Pearson Education, Inc. All rights reserved.

Realidades ①

Episodio 10

Nombre _____

Fecha _____

Hora _____

EPISODIO 10

4.

a. El Inspector Gil dice que "ahora todo es muy lógico."

b. El Inspector Gil dice que "ahora voy a casa."

5.

a. Paco no puede ayudar a Lola con este caso.

b. Paco ayuda a Lola con este caso.

B. Match each quotation from the video with the character who said it. Write the letter of the character's picture and the character's name on the line.

a.   b.   c.   d.

1. "Y los dos son de Barcelona." ___A_____

2. "Luis Antonio tiene mucha suerte." ___A_____

3. "¿Luis Antonio? El hombre del café . . ." ___d_____

4. "María murió, ¿y esta Julia tomó la identidad de María? ¡Es increíble!"

___C_____

5. "No, no fue mi idea. No quería, no quería." ___b_____

C. Who does each statement describe: Lola, María, Luis Antonio, Pedro, or doña Gracia? Some sentences may have more than one answer.

1. Tuvieron un accidente. ___Doña Gracia_____

2. Reconoció a las chicas en el hospital. ___Luis Antonio_____

3. Son novios. ___Lola y Pedro_____

4. Murió en el hospital. ___María_____

5. No puede ver muy bien. _____

© Pearson Education, Inc. All rights reserved.

Realidades 1

Episodio 10

Nombre _____

Fecha _____

Hora _____

EPISODIO 10

6. Vivía con doña Gracia. _Lola_

7. Decide actuar. _Mora_

8. Entra en el piso y ataca a doña Gracia. _Luis Antonio_

9. Lleva las joyas en una maleta. _____

10. Van a salir a cenar. _Lola y Pedro_

D. Write a brief description of each scene from the video below.

1.

_____

2.

_____

3.

_____

4.

_____

© Pearson Education, Inc. All rights reserved.

Realidades ①

Episodio 10

Nombre _____

Hora _____

Fecha _____

EPISODIO 10

E. Read each sentence and write *C* (*cierto*) if it is true or *F* (*falso*) if it is false. If it is false, rewrite the information to make it true.

1. María Requena murió en el accidente de coche. _____
   _____

2. Doña Lupe reconoció a María y a Julia. _____

3. Las dos chicas tenían la misma edad. _____

4. Antes Julia vivía en los Estados Unidos. _____

5. Luis Antonio trabajó en el hospital como enfermero. _____

6. Luis Antonio no reconoce a María. _____

7. María es más alta que Julia. _____

8. La salud de doña Gracia es muy mala. _____

9. Luis Antonio quiere irse a Barcelona. _____

10. Las joyas están en la mochila de Luis Antonio. _____

F. Answer the following questions in complete sentences in Spanish.

1. ¿Quién fue el ladrón? _____

2. ¿Qué le pasó a María? _____

3. ¿Quién resolvió el caso? _____

4. ¿Cómo crees que Julia ayudó a Luis Antonio? _____
   _____

5. ¿Dónde trabajó Luis Antonio? ¿Qué trabajo tenía? _____
   _____

6. ¿Quién sabe que doña Gracia tiene una fortuna? _____
   _____

7. ¿Cuándo ocurrió el robo? ¿Cuántos días pasaron desde que ocurrió el robo hasta solucionarlo? _____

© Pearson Education, Inc. All rights reserved.

8. ¿Con quién sale Lola a cenar al final de este episodio? _____

_____

9. ¿Quién dice que Lola es la mejor detective de Madrid? ¿Y quién dice que es la mejor de Europa? _____

_____

10. Otra vez escuchamos el título del misterio. ¿Quién lo dice? _____

_____

 Para hablar

Work with a partner to decide what you think would happen if there were another episode of *¿Eres tú, María?* Role-play part of this episode, then act it out for the class.

 Para escribir

Write a review of the video for your school newspaper. Describe the main characters and explain the plot—but don't give it all away! Come up with a title for each episode that describes a bit of what happened in each one. You should try to make the readers interested in the video. Explain why you did or did not like it.

© Pearson Education, Inc. All rights reserved.

Realidades ①

Episodio 10

Nombre _____

Hora _____

Fecha _____

EPISODIO 10

Nota cultural

España

Pedro says Lola is the best detective in Madrid. Then Lola says that she's the best in Spain, the best in Europe. How much do you know about Spain?

The mainland of Spain covers about five-sixths of the Iberian Peninsula, which includes Portugal to the east. Spain also has several islands: the Canary Islands off the northwest coast of Africa and the Balearic Islands in the Mediterranean Sea; it also has the North African enclaves of Ceuta and Melilla.

With an area of about 195,000 square miles, Spain is one of the largest European countries; it is three-fourths the size of Texas. Within the country, there is a variety of climatic and topographical conditions.

Seventy-five percent of the mainland is a high, dry plateau called La Meseta. Spain is the second most mountainous country of Europe (Switzerland is first). The greater part of the population lives either in the capital city of Madrid (the geographical, political, and cultural center of the nation) or along one of the fertile coastal plains.

Most of Spain lies along the same latitudes as Maine and Virginia. Spain is generally sunnier, drier, and warmer than those areas because of its topography and the effect of the warm Mediterranean currents.

Have you ever been to Spain? If so, what did you like and dislike? If not, would you like to? Why or why not?

_____

_____

_____

_____

_____

© Pearson Education, Inc. All rights reserved.

Realidades 1

Episodio 10

Nombre

Fecha

Hora

EPISODIO 10

Para explorar en Internet

Now, go online to research one of the following topics about Spain: history, economy, education, government, lifestyle, food, or recreation. Share your findings with the rest of the class.

© Pearson Education, Inc. All rights reserved.

Vocabulario español-inglés

A dash (—) represents the main entry word. For example, — **mismo** after **ahora** means **ahora mismo**.

A

a to (*prep.*)
    — **la una de la mañana** at one in the morning
    ¿— **qué hora?** (at) what time?
    — **ver** let's see
el **abogado, la abogada** lawyer
abrir to open
el **abuelo, la abuela** grandfather, grandmother
acabar de + *inf.* . . . to have just . . .
    Acabo de hablar con . . . I just spoke with . . .
    Acabo de venir del hospital. I just came from the hospital.
    Acabo de ver . . . I just saw . . .
el **accidente** accident
    — **de coche** car accident
acerca de about
acordarse de (o → ue) to remember
actuar to act
adiós good-bye
el **agua** (*f.*) water
ahora now
    — **mismo** right away
¡ajá! aha!
al (a + el), a la to the
    — **día siguiente** the next day
    — **lado de** next to
la **alegría** happiness, joy
algo something
    — **así** something like that
alguien someone
allá there
allí there
alto, -a tall
la **altura** height
amable kind
la **ambulancia** ambulance
el **amigo, la amiga** friend
el **andén** (train) platform
el **año** year
anoche last night
antes de before
aparecer to appear
aquí here
el **archivo** file, records
el **arte** art
atacar to attack
¡Ay de mí! Oh no!, Woe is me!
ayer yesterday
la **ayuda** help
ayudar to help
azul blue

B

el **balcón** balcony
basta de that's enough of
    — **detective por hoy.** That's enough of being a detective today.
bastante enough
bien well
    ¿**Está** —? Is that all right?
bonito, -a pretty
buenas tardes good afternoon
bueno well, all right (*adv.*)
bueno (buen), -a good (*adj.*)
buenos días good morning
buscar to look for
    buscamos we're looking for

C

la **cabeza** head
el **café** coffee; café
la **calle** street
calmarse to calm down
    cálmate take it easy, calm down (*fam. command*)
    cálmese take it easy, calm down (*form. command*)
la **cárcel** jail
la **carretera** highway
la **carta** letter
la **casa** home
casi almost
el **caso** case
la **casualidad** coincidence, chance
    ¡Que —! What a coincidence!
cenar to have dinner
cerca (de) close (to), near
el **chico, la chica** boy, girl
chocar to crash
los **churros** fried dough pastries
la **cita** appointment; date
claro of course
    — **que sí** of course
el **cliente, la clienta** client
cobrar to charge
el **coche** car
colgar (o → ue) to hang up (the telephone)
el **collar de perlas** pearl necklace
comer to eat
la **comida** meal; lunch
¿cómo? how?, what?
    ¿— **está?** How is she/he? How are you? (*form., sing.*)
    ¿— **está doña Gracia?** How is doña Gracia?
    ¿— **estas?** How are you? (*fam., sing.*)
el **compañero, la compañera de habitación** roommate
comprender to understand
con with

conmigo with me
contigo with you
conocer to know
contento, -a happy
contratar to contract, to hire
correr to run
correspondiente corresponding
la **cosa** thing
creer to think, to believe
    creo que sí I think so
el **crimen** crime
¿Cuál es tu dirección (electrónica)? What's your e-mail address?
¿Cuál es tu número de teléfono? What's your phone number?
cuando when
    — **quiera** whenever you want
¿cuándo? when?
curioso, -a strange, curious

D

de of, from
    — **acuerdo** agreed, OK
    delante — in front of
    — **la mañana** in the morning (*with time*)
    — **la noche** in the evening (*with time*)
    — **la tarde** in the afternoon (*with time*)
    — **muy buena salud** in very good health
    — **nada** you're welcome
    ¿— **parte de quién?** Who's calling?
    ¿— **qué tipo?** What kind?
enfrente — in front of
deber should, must
    debe de ser it should be
    debes ir you should go
decidir to decide
decir to say, to tell
del (de + el), de la of the
delante de in front of
delgado, -a thin
demasiado too, too much
el **deporte** sport
desafortunadamente unfortunately
desaparecer to disappear
describir to describe
la **descripción** description
descubrir to discover
desear to want
después (de) after
el, la **detective** detective
    — **privado, -a** private detective
detener to stop; to arrest
    ¡Deténgala! Arrest her!
el **día** day

el **diamante** diamond
dice he/she/it says; you (*form., sing.*) say
difícil difficult, hard
dígame tell me (*form. command*)
dime tell me (*fam. command*)
el **dinero** money
¡Dios mío! Goodness gracious!
la **dirección** address
disculpa excuse me
el **domingo** Sunday
don, doña *title of respect before a person's first name*
donde where
¿dónde? where?
dormir (o → ue) to sleep
el **dormitorio** bedroom
Dos coches chocaron . . . Two cars crashed . . .

E
la **edad** age
el **edificio** building
el, la the
El ladrón robó . . . The robber stole . . .
él he
  Él les ayudó a los dos. He helped the two of them.
  Él no conoce a su abuela. He doesn't know his grandmother.
  Él pierde la paciencia. He loses his patience.
elegante elegant
ella she
  Ella las perdió. She lost them.
en in, on, at
  — realidad really
  — seguida at once, immediately
encantado, -a delighted
encantar to please very much, to love
  a él/ella le encanta(n) he/she loves
  me encantaría . . . I would love to . . .
encontrar (o → ue) to find
el **enfermero, la enfermera** nurse
enfermo, -a sick
enfrente (de) in front (of)
entonces then
entrar en to enter (in), to go inside
entre between, among
era he/she it was; you (*form., sing.*) were
eran they/you (*form., pl.*) were
el **error** mistake
es he/she/it is; you (*form., sing.*) are
  — la una it's one o'clock
  — mi caso it's my case

— raro it's strange
la **escena** scene
escribir to write
escuchar to listen (to)
ese, esa that
la **esmeralda** emerald
eso that (*neuter*)
  — parece that's what it seems like
esperar to wait
el **esposo, la esposa** husband, wife
está aquí he's/she's here
¿Está bien? Is that all right?
esta noche tonight
estaba he/she/it was; you (*form., sing.*) were
estaban they/you (*form., pl.*) were
la **estación** station
estamos buscándola we're looking for her
estar to be
  — de vacaciones to be on vacation
  — seguro, -a to be sure
¿Estás segura? Are you sure? (*fam., sing., f.*)
este, esta this
esto this (*neuter*)
estuvo he/she/it was; you (*form., sing.*) were
  — aquí . . . He/She was here . . .
  — en un accidente. He/She was in an accident.
el **euro** *currency used by some countries in the European Union*
evidente evident
exacto, -a exact
existir to exist
explicar to explain
extraño, -a strange

F
fácil easy
la **familia** family
fantástico, -a fantastic
la **fortuna** fortune
la **foto** photo
la **frase** sentence
fue (*preterite of ir & ser*) he/she/it went/was; you (*form., sing.*) went/were
fueron (*preterite of ir & ser*) they/you (*form., pl.*) went/were
fui (*preterite of ir & ser*) I went/was

G
los **gastos** expenses
el **golpe** hit, blow
gracias thank you
grave serious

guapo, -a handsome, pretty
gustar to like
  a él/ella le gusta(n) he/she likes
  (a mí) me gusta(n) I like
  me gustaría . . . I would like to . . .

H
la **habitación** room; bedroom
hablar to speak, to talk
¿Habló del incidente? Did he/she talk about the incident?
hace + *time expression* ago
  — dos días two days ago
hacer to make; to do
hasta until
  — ahora until now
  — luego see you later
hay there is, there are
el **hermano, la hermana** brother, sister
el **hijo, la hija** son, daughter
la **historia** story
el **historial clínico** hospital record
hola hello
el **hombre** man
el **hospital** hospital
hoy today

I
iba a she/he/it was going to; you (*form., sing.*) were going to
la **idea** idea
la **identidad** identity
importante important
importar to matter
  a él/ella le importa it matters to him/her
imposible impossible
el **incidente** incident
increíble incredible
indicar to indicate, to show
la **información** information
inmediatamente immediately
el **inspector, la inspectora** inspector
interesante interesting
interesar to interest
  a él/ella le interesa(n) he/she is interested in
el **investigador, la investigadora** investigator
investigar to investigate
ir to go
  — a + *inf.* to be going to + *verb*
irse to go away

J
las **joyas** jewelry, jewels
juntos, -as together

L
La cuenta, por favor. The check, please.

el   **ladrón, la ladrona** thief, robber
     las reconoció he/she recognized
        them
la   **leche** milk
     leer to read
     listo, -a ready
     llamar to call; to knock (*on a*
        door)
        — por teléfono to telephone
     llamarse to be called
        me llamo my name is
        se llama his/her name is
la   **llave** key
     llegar to arrive
     llevados, -as taken
     llevar to carry, to take
     lo que what
     lo sé I know
     lo siento I'm sorry
     lógico, -a logical
     luego later

M • • • • • • • • • • • • • • • •
     magnífico magnificent
     mal bad, badly (*adv.*)
la   **maleta** suitcase
     malo (mal), -a bad (*adj.*)
     María tenía las llaves. María had
        the keys.
     más more
        — tarde later
     mayor old, older
     me me (*dir. & indir. obj.*)
        — gustaría I would like
        — voy I'm going, I'm leaving
el   **médico, la médica** doctor
     mejor better
el   **mes** month
     mi my
     mí me (*after prep.*)
el   **miembro** member
el   **minuto** minute
     mío, -a mine
     mirar to look (at), to see
        mira look (*fam. command*)
        mire look (*form. command*)
     mismo, -a same; very
     misterioso, -a mysterious
la   **mochila** backpack
el, **la modelo** model
el   **momento** moment
     moreno, -a brown (*of hair color*)
     morir (o → ue) to die
     mostrar (o → ue) to show
     mucha suerte a lot of luck
     muchas gracias thank you very
        much
     mucho much (*adv.*)
        — mejor much better
     mucho, -a much (*adj.*)
     muchos, -as many
la   **muerte** death
     muerto, -a dead
la   **mujer** woman

     murió he/she/it/you (*form.,
        sing.*) died
     muy very
     — bien very well

N • • • • • • • • • • • • • • • •
     nada nothing
     necesario, -a necessary
     necesitar to need; to have to
        Necesito saber . . . I need to
        know . . .
     ni . . . ni neither . . . nor
el   **nieto, la nieta** grandson,
        granddaughter
     ninguno, -a none (*adj.*)
     no no; not
        **— estoy pensando
        en . . .** I'm not planning
        to . . .
        **— hay absolutamente nada
        sobre María Requena.**
        There is absolutely
        nothing about María
        Requena.
        — la conozco. I don't know
        her.
        — lo sé. I don't know.
        — me diga you don't say
        (*form., sing.*)
        ¡— me sigas! Don't follow
        me! (*fam. command*)
        — puede ver bien. She can't
        see well.
        — quería. I didn't want to.
        — quiere esperar (he/she)
        doesn't want to wait
        — sé qué hacer I don't know
        what to do
        — ve casi nada. He/She can
        hardly see anything.
        — viene a trabajar. He/She
        hasn't been coming to
        work.
        — viene nunca aquí.
        He/She never comes
        here.
la   **noche** night
        esta — tonight
el   **nombre** name
     nosotros, -as we; us
        — cobramos . . . We
        charge . . .
las **noticias** news
los **novios** girlfriend and boyfriend
     nuevo, -a new
el   **número** number

O • • • • • • • • • • • • • • • •
     observar to observe
     ocurrir to occur, to happen
la   **oficina** office
     olvidar to forget
la   **oportunidad** opportunity
el   **orden** order

     en — in order
     otra vez again
     otro, -a other, another
     oye he/she/it hears; you (*form.,
        sing.*) hear; listen (*fam.
        command*)

P • • • • • • • • • • • • • • • •
la   **paciencia** patience
el, **la paciente** patient
el   **padre** father
     pagar to pay (for)
el   **papel** paper
     para for
        ¿— qué? for what?
        — ti for you (*fam., sing.*)
     parecer to seem
     pasado, -a last
     pasar to happen; to spend (*time*)
     **Pasó antes de venir a vivir con
     doña Gracia.** It happened
        before she came to live with
        doña Gracia.
     Pasó tres meses . . . He/She
        spent three months . . .
el   **pelo** hair
     pensar (e → ie) to think
     perder (e → ie) to lose
     perdón excuse me
     perdona excuse me (*fam.
        command*)
     perdóneme excuse me, pardon
        me (*form. command*)
el   **periódico** newspaper
el, **la periodista** journalist,
        newspaper reporter
las **perlas** pearls
     pero but
la   **persona** person
el   **personaje** character (*of a book,
        movie, play*)
el   **piso** apartment; floor (*of a
        building*)
la   **planta** plant
la   **plaza** (town) square
     ¡Pobrecita! Poor thing! (*f.*)
     poder (o → ue) to be able, can
el, **la policía** police officer; (*f.*) police
        force
     por for, by
        ¡— Dios! Oh my God!
        — eso that's why
        — favor please
        — fin finally
        — hoy for today
        — la mañana in the
        morning
        — la noche in the evening,
        at night
     ¿por qué? why?
     porque because
     posible possible
     precioso, -a precious, beautiful
la   **pregunta** question

preguntar to question, to ask questions

   — por to ask about

preocuparse to worry

presentar to present

presentarse to introduce oneself

primero, -a first

privado, -a private

el **problema** problem

la **profesión** profession

profesional professional

pronto soon

la **puerta** door

pues well, then

Q • • • • • • • •

que who, that

¿qué? what?

¡qué + *adj.***!** How . . . !

   ¡— bien! That's great!

   ¡— casualidad! What a coincidence!

   ¿— debo hacer? What should I do?

   ¿— desea beber? What do you want to drink?

   ¡— desgracia! What a misfortune!

   ¡— día! What a day!

   — en paz descanse may he/she rest in peace

   ¿— es esto? What's this?

   ¿— hay de nuevo? What's new?

   ¡— horror! How dreadful!

   ¡— lástima! What a shame!

   ¿— le pasó a ella? What happened to her?

   ¿— pasa? What's going on? What's happening?

   ¿— pasó? What happened?

   ¿— tal? How are you? What's up?

querer (e → ie) to want

   — saber to want to know

quería he/she/it/you *(form., sing.)* wanted

¿quién? who?

   ¿— era? Who was he/she?

quiere irse he/she wants to go away

quiero I want

   — investigate . . . I want to investigate . . .

quisiera I would like

R • • • • • • • •

rápidamente quickly *(adv.)*

rápido, -a fast, quick *(adj.)*

raro, -a strange

el **recado** message

recibir to receive

la **recompensa** reward

reconocer to recognize

recordar (o → ue) to remember

recuerdos greetings, regards

repetir (e → i) to repeat

el **resumen** summary

la **revista** magazine

rico, -a rich

robar to steal, rob

   robarlas to steal them

   ¿Robaron . . . ? Did they steal . . . ?

S • • • • • • • •

el **sábado** Saturday

   el — pasado last Saturday

saber to know (how to)

   no sé qué hacer I don't know what to do

   yo (no) sé I (don't) know

   ¿Sabe . . . ? Does he/she know . . . ?

salir to leave, to go out

la **salud** health

   estar de muy buena — to be in very good health

el **secretario, la secretaria** secretary

el **secreto** secret

seguir to follow

   ¡No me sigas! Don't follow me! *(fam. command)*

el **segundo** second

   un — just a minute

seguro, -a sure

sentarse to sit down

sepa (that) I/he/she/it/you/ *(form, sing.)* know *(subjunctive)*

ser to be

si if

sí yes

   —me acuerdo de María. Yes, I remember María.

siempre always

sobre about

el **sobrino, la sobrina** nephew, niece

Sólo recuerda . . . He/She only remembers . . .

solucionar to solve

soy I am

su his, her, its, your *(form., sing. & pl.)*, their

   — sobrina her niece

el **suelo** floor

la **suerte** luck

   ¡Suerte! Good luck!

suficiente sufficient, enough

suyo, -a yours *(form., sing. & pl.)*, his, hers, theirs

T • • • • • • • •

tal such, such a

talento talent

también also, too

tampoco neither

tarde late *(adv.)*

la **tarde** afternoon

la **tarjeta** card

   — postal postcard

¿Te acuerdas de ella? Do you remember her?

¿Te acuerdas de María Requena? Do you remember María Requena?

el **teléfono** telephone

la **televisión** television

tener to have

   — años to be — years old

   — razón to be right

Tengo que colgar. I have to hang up.

tenía he/she/it/you *(form., sing.)* had

   — un secretario. He/She had a secretary.

Tiene 85 años. He's/She's 85 years old.

tercer(o), -a third

terrible terrible

el **tiempo** time

todavía still

todo, -a all

tomar to take; to drink

   — nota to take note

trabajar to work

el **trabajo** work

el **transporte** transportation

triste sad

tu your *(fam., sing.)*

tú you *(fam., sing.)*

tuvieron they/you *(form., pl.)* had

Tuvo problemas con él. He/She had problems with him.

U • • • • • • • •

último, -a last

un, una a, an; one

único, -a only

unos, -as some

usted you *(form., sing.)*

ustedes you *(form., pl.)*

V • • • • • • • •

va he/she/it goes; you *(form., sing.)* go

   ¿— a comer algo? Are you going to eat something?

   — a recibir . . . She's going to receive . . .

vale OK

valioso, -a valuable

el **valor** value

¡Vamos! Let's go!

vamos a ver let's see

ve a sentarte go sit *(fam. command)*

venir to come

venga come *(form. command)*

vengan en seguida come right away (*form. pl. command*)
venid come (**vosotros** *command*)
ver to see
    ve he/she/it sees; you (*form., sing.*) see
    vi (preterite of *ver*) I saw
    Vi a su abuela. I saw your (*form., sing.*) grandmother.
la **verdad** truth
    ¿Verdad? Really?
verdadero, -a true, real
la **vez** time
    otra — again

la **víctima** victim
    viejo, -a old
la **visita** visitor
visitar to visit
vivir to live
    vivía he/she/it/you (*form., sing.*) used to live
volver (o → ue) to return
    — a + *inf.* to do something again (**volver a leer** to read again)
voy I go, I'm going
    — a pensarlo. I'll think about it.

Y • • • • • • • • • • • • • • • •
y and
ya already
yo I
    — fui a visitarla. I went to visit her.
    — mismo, -a I myself